Almighty God,
to you all hearts are open,
all desires known,
and from you no secrets are hid:
Cleanse the thoughts of our hearts
by the inspiration of your Holy Spirit,
that we may perfectly love you,
and worthily magnify your holy Name;
through Christ our Lord.
Amen.

First published in Great Britain by

Movement for the Ordination of Women

First American edition published by

Morehouse-Barlow Co., Inc.
78 Danbury Road, Wilton, Connecticut 06897

ISBN: 0-8192-1443-4

Printed in the United States of America
by
BSC Litho, Harrisburg, PA

Design/print
GregoryDesign
West Hallam
Derbyshire

Contents

Preface

'All desires known': this phrase has always evoked in me that distinctive stance which I associate with authentic worship: namely, an appalled sense of self-exposure combined with a curious but profound relief; and so to write under this title has been both a discipline and a comfort. I have chosen it because I understand the Christian life to be about the integration of desire: our personal desires, our political vision, and our longing for God. So far from being separate or in competition with one another, I believe that our deepest desires ultimately spring from the same source; and worship is the place where this can be acknowledged.

I have also tried, in my writing, to integrate my faith and my feminism. For me, as for many others in recent years, the women's movement has been the place where my Christian faith has been most strongly challenged, and yet has also been the most important resource for its renewed growth and energy. At the same time, the persistently subversive character of the gospel operates to prevent the feminist struggle for the empowerment of women from turning into one more ideology of self-justification.

In worship, our ideologies stand exposed, and nowhere is this clearer than in the assumptions expressed in our language. Increasingly, the convention by which God has been addressed in terms that are exclusively male has caused discomfort among worshippers; but the problem of finding new words is not simple. There is often something unsatisfactory about altering existing texts to make them 'sound'. In any case, the effort to erase gender from our image of God, or to make everything fair and balanced, can produce linguistic awkwardness and tend towards a neutrality in prayer which I think is inappropriate. Much more potentially creative is the writing of new texts in vigorous language, which also respects and inhabits ancient worship forms, evocative biblical imagery, and familiar cadences and rhythms.

'Inclusive language' does not have to mean replacing 'Almighty Father' with an (equally problematic) 'Almighty Mother'. I have found that to examine how and why the feminine has been omitted from our ways of addressing God is to discover also what else has been left out. To release ourselves from the habit of always using certain predictable (and perhaps scarcely-noticed) formulae for the beginning of a prayer, may free the imagination to explore the unimaginable ways in which God reaches us. At the same time, the very range of possible imagery forbids us to *identify* God with any limited form of words. We have a model for this practice in the Hebrew psalms, and in the long but often submerged tradition of Christian mysticism. In both, we find not only a wealth of exuberant but provisional imagery, but also a distinctive blend of the passionate and the political, that can express the integration of our desire.

In some of my prayers, particularly towards the end of this book, I do use explicitly feminine imagery for God. This is not because I seek to worship a 'goddess'—any more than generations of calling God 'He' implies belief in a literally male 'god'. It is that I have come to acknowledge how profoundly the women friends whom I love and struggle with have helped me to articulate my longings, and have mediated the love of God to me. But I also recognize that if, as women, our only access to the *strangeness* of God is through the 'otherness' of the male image, then that will insist on the wrong kind of otherness; and it may encourage us to avoid some of the more painful and intimate dilemmas of religious belief. Feminine imagery not only affirms a comfortable closeness for women to the God in whose image we are made: it also prevents us from distancing ourselves—as we can do with 'male' language—from the uncomfortable, even frightening closeness of the difficult God who is not made in our image.

The collects. These are a complete series of collects for Sundays and major week-day festivals, and a selection of collects for lesser festivals and other occasional uses. They were written week by week over the course of one lectionary year, from Advent 1986 to Advent 1987, in association with the eucharistic lectionary of the Church of England's Alternative Service Book, 1980.* Some are closely tied in with the precise stage of the liturgical year; others, while related to the set theme, will also be usable in other contexts and at other times. In most cases, the collect will link more strongly with one or two of the set readings than with the others. To indicate these, and for the convenience of those wanting to use the prayers independently of the ASB, I have made marginal references. Other relevant biblical passages which are not set in the lectionary are shown in brackets; but the notes are not exhaustive. The collects are designed to have a wide use in church and elsewhere, and their language is deliberately inclusive. However, wherever possible within the constraints of the lectionary, I have picked up images and narratives concerning women, as norms for the Christian life.

The formal prayers. These are written in various traditional forms: litany, canticle, eucharistic prayer, confession, blessing. Some are linked to specific or festival use; others will be adaptable to a range of settings. Some are more suitable for women's groups; others presuppose a mixed congregation. Virtually all were written initially for a particular occasion of use by a worshipping group, and I have indicated this as appropriate. Theologically, it will be noted that I frequently refer to the Wisdom of God, who is personified in feminine terms in an important strand of Jewish thought. Strong and significant echoes of the Wisdom tradition in fact underlie many of the crucial Christological passages of the New Testament. The eucharistic prayers in this section aim to combine traditional Christian theology of the eucharist with a special emphasis on, and celebration for, the witness of women in the life of Jesus.

The psalms and poems. The genre of psalm is particularly interesting from a feminist point of view, since it allows for an intense individuality of utterance which, because of how psalms have always been used, can nevertheless convey a communal voice. Hence it is an excellent form for expressing the perception that the personal is political; and the ancient heritage of the psalm carries considerable authority of tone.

However, because of the (still unusual) feminine language for God, and because of the intimacy of the material in this section, I recommend that the psalms and poems should only be introduced into group worship if careful thought has been given about their appropriateness. Women can feel peculiarly exposed by this language, and may understandably resent its being imposed without preparation. It is valuable to include opportunity for discussion, where mixed feelings can be explored.

The material in this collection, though written quite recently, has been gestating a long time, and it has been called out and supported by a community. I now offer it to a wider one; and in writing these prayers for public and private worship, I have attempted to leave 'space' within the words for those meanings which can only be created by each particular constellation of place, time, and people who want to use them in the presence of God.

Janet Morley, Advent 1987

**Available in the United States through Morehouse-Barlow.*

Collects

9 before Christmas

Holy Spirit,
mighty wind of God,
inhabit our darkness
brood over our abyss
and speak to our chaos;
that we may breathe with your life
and share your creation
in the power of Jesus Christ, Amen.

Genesis 1 and 2
Creation

8 before Christmas

Holy God,
we are born into a world
tissued and structured by sin.
When we proclaim our innocence
and seek to accuse each other,
give us the grace to know that we are naked;
that we may cry out to you alone
through Jesus Christ, Amen.

Genesis 3.1-15
Fall
Genesis 4.1-10
Cain and Abel
Romans 7.7-13
(1 John 1.5-10)

7 before Christmas

Fearful God,
you require of our love
appalling sacrifice;
and your lasting promise
is contained in contradiction.
May we so lay on your altar
our dearest desires
that we may receive them back from you
as unaccountable gift,
through Jesus Christ, Amen.

Genesis 22.
1-18
Abraham and Isaac
(Mark 8.34-5)

6 before Christmas

God whose holy name
defies our definition,
but whose will is known
in freeing the oppressed,
make us to be one
with all who cry for justice;
that we who speak your praise
may struggle for your truth,
through Jesus Christ, Amen.

Exodus 3.7-15
I AM WHO I AM

1 Kings 19.
9-18
Elijah and the still small voice.

O God from whom we flee,
whose stillness is more terrible
than earthquake, wind, or fire,
speak to our loneliness
and challenge our despair;
that in your very absence
we may recognize your voice,
and wrapped in your presence
we may go forth to encounter the world,
in the name of Christ, Amen.

5 before Christmas

1 Thessalonians
5.1-11
(Mark 13.
8-end)
(Romans 8.
18-25)

God our deliverer,
whose approaching birth
still shakes the foundations of our world,
may we so wait for your coming
with eagerness and hope
that we embrace without terror
the labour pangs of the new age,
through Jesus Christ, Amen.

Advent Sunday

Isaiah 55.1-11
Luke 4.14-21
Sermon at Nazareth
Timothy 3.14-
4.5

O God our disturber,
whose speech is pregnant with power
and whose word will be fulfilled;
may we know ourselves unsatisfied
with all that distorts your truth,
and make our hearts attentive
to your liberating voice,
in Jesus Christ, Amen.

Advent 2

Isaiah 40.1-11
Malachi 3.1-5

God our healer,
whose mercy is like a refining fire,
touch us with your judgement,
and confront us with your tenderness;
that, being comforted by you,
we may reach out to a troubled world,
through Jesus Christ, Amen.

Advent 3

Advent 4 Annunciation

O unknown God,
whose presence is announced
not among the impressive
but in obscurity;
come, overshadow us now,
and speak to our hidden places;
that, entering your darkness with joy,
we may choose to cooperate with you,
through Jesus Christ, Amen.

Luke 1.26-38 *Annunciation*
1 Corinthians 1. 26-end

Christmas Eve Christmas Day

God our beloved,
born of a woman's body:
you came that we might look upon you,
and handle you with our own hands.
May we so cherish one another in our bodies
that we may also be touched by you;
through the Word made flesh, Jesus Christ,
Amen.

John 1.1-14
(1 John 1.1-4)

Christmas 1

Loving Word of God,
you have shown us the fullness of your glory
in taking human flesh.
Fill us, in our bodily life,
with your grace and truth;
that our pleasure may be boundless,
and our integrity complete,
in your name, Amen.

John 1.14-18

Christmas 2

God of community,
whose call is more insistent
than ties of family or blood;
may we so respect and love
those whose lives are linked with ours
that we fail not in loyalty to you,
but make choices according to your will,
through Jesus Christ, Amen.

Luke 2.41-end *Child Jesus in the Temple*
(Mark 3. 31-end) *Jesus' true family*

Matthew 2. 1-12
Visit of the Magi

Epiphany

O God, the source of all insight,
whose coming was revealed to the nations
not among men of power
but on a woman's lap;
give us grace to seek you
where you may be found,
that the wisdom of this world may be humbled
and discover your unexpected joy,
through Jesus Christ, Amen.

Isaiah 42.1-7
Matthew 3. 13-end
Jesus' baptism
(Joel 2.28-9)

Epiphany 1

Spirit of energy and change,
in whose power Jesus was anointed
to be the hope of the nations;
be poured out also upon us
without reserve or distinction,
that we may have confidence and strength
to plant your justice on the earth,
through Jesus Christ, Amen.

Acts 26.9-20
Galatians 1. 11-end
Conversion of Paul
(2 Corinthians 12.7-10)

Epiphany 2
Conversion of Paul

O God against whom we struggle,
you speak with the voice of the persecuted
and call the oppressor to turn to you;
confront in us the violence
that we enact or consent to,
that our strength may be made perfect
in weakness,
and we may put our trust in you,
through Jesus Christ, Amen.

Exodus 33. 12-end
Moses in the cleft of the rock

Epiphany 3

O God,
whose beauty is beyond our imagining
and whose power we cannot comprehend;
show us your glory
as far as we can grasp it,
and shield us
from knowing more than we can bear
until we may look upon you without fear,
through Jesus Christ, Amen.

Epiphany 4

Holy God,
whose presence is known
in the structures we build,
and also in their collapse;
establish in us a community of hope,
not to contain your mystery,
but to be led beyond security
into your sacred space,
through Jesus Christ, Amen.

1 Kings 8. 22-30 *Solomon's prayer*
1 Corinthians 3.10-17
John 2.13-22 *Jesus cleanses the temple*
Jeremiah 7. 1-11

Epiphany 5

Hidden God,
whose wisdom compels our love
and unsettles all our values;
fill us with desire
to search for her truth,
that we may transform the world
becoming fools for her sake,
through Jesus Christ, Amen.

Proverbs 2.1-9
1 Corinthians 3.18-end

Epiphany 6

Christ our teacher,
you reach into our lives
not through instruction, but story.
Open our hearts to be attentive;
that seeing, we may perceive,
and hearing, we may understand,
and understanding, may act upon your word,
in your name, Amen.

Parables (Mark 4.1-20)

9 before Easter

Vulnerable God,
you challenge the powers that rule this world
through the needy, the compassionate,
and those who are filled with longing.
Make us hunger and thirst to see right prevail,
and single-minded in seeking peace;
that we may see your face
and be satisfied in you,
through Jesus Christ, Amen.

1 Corinthians 4.8-13
Matthew 5. 1-12 *Beatitudes*
1 Corinthians 2.1-10

Mark 7.24-end
Syro-Phoenician woman

O God whose word is life,
and whose delight is to answer our cry,
give us faith like the Syro-Phoenician woman,
who refused to remain an outsider;
that we too may have the wit to argue
and demand that our daughters be made whole,
through Jesus Christ, Amen.

8 before Easter

Mark 2.13-17
John 8.2-11
Woman taken in adultery

Christ our companion,
you came not to humiliate the sinner
but to disturb the righteous.
Welcome us when we are put to shame,
but challenge our smugness,
that we may truly turn from what is evil,
and be freed even from our virtues,
in your name, Amen.

7 before Easter

Isaiah 58.1-8
Matthew 6.16-21

O God,
you have made us for yourself,
and against your longing there is no defence.
Mark us with your love,
and release in us a passion for your justice
in our disfigured world;
that we may turn from our guilt and face you,
our heart's desire,
Amen.

Ash Wednesday

Matthew 4.1-11
Luke 4.1-13
(Mark 1.12-13)
The Temptations

Spirit of integrity,
you drive us into the desert
to search out our truth.
Give us clarity to know what is right,
and courage to reject what is strategic;
that we may abandon the false innocence
of failing to choose at all,
but may follow the purposes of Jesus Christ,
Amen.

Lent 1

Lent 2

Spirit of truth and judgement,
who alone can exorcize
the powers that grip our world;
at the point of crisis
give us your discernment,
that we may accurately name what is evil,
and know the way that leads to peace,
through Jesus Christ, Amen.

1 John 4.1-6
Luke 19. 41-end
Jesus weeps over Jerusalem
Matthew 12. 22-32

Lent 3

Jesus our brother,
you followed the necessary path
and were broken on our behalf.
May we neither cling to our pain
where it is futile,
nor refuse to embrace the cost
when it is required of us;
that in losing our selves for your sake,
we may be brought to new life,
Amen.

Luke 9.18-27
Matthew 16v13-end
(Mark 8. 27-end)
Peter's confession

Lent 4
Mothering Sunday

God our mother,
you hold our life within you;
nourish us at your breast,
and teach us to walk alone.
Help us so to receive your tenderness
and respond to your challenge
that others may draw life from us,
in your name, Amen.

(Isaiah 46.3-4
49.14-16
66.7-13
Hosea 11.1-4)

For collect linked to ASB readings, see Transfiguration, p.26

Lent 5
Passion Sunday

Christ our Lord,
you refused the way of domination
and died the death of a slave.
May we also refuse to lord it
over those who are subject to us,
but share the weight of authority
so that all may be empowered
in your name, Amen.

Mark 10.32-45
Who is the greatest?

O God, the source of our passion,
who took upon you our unprotected flesh,
kindle in us
your anger and desire;
that in suffering we may not be consumed,
but hold fast to you
through Jesus Christ, Amen.

Lent 6
Palm Sunday

Matthew 21. 1-13
(Luke 19. 28-40)
Triumphal entry
Mark 14. 32-15.41
Passion narrative

God, our hope of victory
whom we constantly betray;
grant us so to recognize your coming
that in our clamour
there may be commitment,
and in our silence
the very stones may cry aloud
in your name, Amen.

Maundy Thursday

(John 12.1-11)
Anointing at Bethany
John 13.1-15
Jesus washes his disciples' feet

Christ, whose feet were caressed
with perfume and a woman's hair;
you humbly took basin and towel
and washed the feet of your friends.
Wash us also in your tenderness
as we touch one another;
that, embracing your service freely,
we may accept no other bondage
in your name, Amen.

Good Friday

Isaiah 52. 13-53-end
Suffering Servant
John 18. 1-19.37
Passion narrative

Christ our victim,
whose beauty was disfigured
and whose body torn upon the cross;
open wide your arms
to embrace our tortured world,
that we may not turn away our eyes,
but abandon ourselves to your mercy,
Amen.

Christ, whose bitter agony
was watched from afar by women,
enable us to follow the example
of their persistent love;
that, being steadfast in the face of horror,
we may also know the place of resurrection,
in your name, Amen.

(Mark 15. 40-16.1)
Witness of the women

Easter Eve

O God,
you have searched the depths we cannot know,
and touched what we cannot bear to name;
may we so wait,
enclosed in your darkness,
that we are ready to encounter
the terror of the dawn,
with Jesus Christ, Amen.

Job 14.1-14
(Psalm 139)

Easter Day

God of terror and joy,
you arise to shake the earth.
Open our graves
and give us back the past;
so that all that has been buried
may be freed and forgiven,
and our lives may return to you
through the risen Christ, Amen.

(Matthew 27.51-54)
Matthew 28. 1-10
Resurrection
(Isaiah 2. 19-21)
Mark 16.1-8
The women's fear

O unfamiliar God,
we seek you in the places
you have already left,
and fail to see you
even when you stand before us.
Grant us so to recognize your strangeness
that we need not cling to our familiar grief,
but may be freed to proclaim resurrection
in the name of Christ, Amen.

John 20.1-18
Mary Magdalene at the tomb

(Luke 24.1-11)
Women disbelieved

O God, the power of the powerless,
you have chosen as your witnesses
those whose voice is not heard.
Grant that, as women first announced
the resurrection
though they were not believed,
we too may have courage
to persist in proclaiming your word,
in the power of Jesus Christ, Amen.

John 20.19-29
Doubting Thomas

Easter 1

Risen Christ,
whose absence leaves us paralysed,
but whose presence is overwhelming,
breathe on us
with your abundant life;
that where we cannot see
we may have courage to believe
that we may be raised with you,
Amen.

Luke 24.13-35
Road to Emmaus

Easter 2

O God whose greeting we miss
and whose departure we delay,
make our hearts burn with insight
on our ordinary road;
that, as we grasp you in the broken bread,
we may also let you go,
and return to speak your word of life
in the name of Christ, Amen.

John 11.17-27
Martha's confession

Easter 3

O God,
you call us to commitment
even at the point of despair.
Give us the faith of Martha
to find in our anger and loss
a truthful place to proclaim you
our resurrection and life,
through Jesus Christ, Amen.

Easter 4

Christ our friend,
you ask for our love
in spite of our betrayal.
Give us courage to embrace forgiveness,
know you again,
and trust ourselves in you,
Amen.

John 21.15-22
Jesus and Peter

Easter 5

O God for whom we long
as a woman in labour
longs for her delivery;
give us courage to wait,
strength to push,
and discernment to know the right time;
that we may bring into the world
your joyful peace,
through Jesus Christ, Amen.

John 16.12-24
(Romans 8.
18-25)

Ascension Day

O God,
you withdraw from our sight
that you may be known by our love;
help us to enter the cloud
where you are hidden,
and surrender all our certainty
to the darkness of faith
in Jesus Christ, Amen.

Acts 1.1-11
Ascension

Sunday after Ascension

Christ our lover
to whom we try to cling;
as you have reached into our depths
and drawn us to love you,
so make us open, freely to let you go;
that you may return in unexpected power
to change the world through us,
in your name, Amen.

Luke 24.45-end

Acts 2.1-21
Pentecost
John 14.15-26
John 20.19-23

Pentecost (Whit Sunday)

Spirit of truth
whom the world can never grasp,
touch our hearts
with the shock of your coming;
fill us with desire
for your disturbing peace;
and fire us with longing
to speak your uncontainable word
through Jesus Christ, Amen.

Pentecost 1 (Trinity Sunday)

O God our mystery,
you bring us to life,
call us to freedom,
and move between us with love.
May we so participate
in the dance of your trinity,
that our lives may resonate with you,
now and for ever, Amen.

Luke 14.15-24
Parable of the dinner party
1 Peter 2.1-10
Acts 2.37-end
(Ephesians 2. 19-20)

Pentecost 2

O God, at whose table
we are no longer strangers;
may we not refuse your call
through pride or fear,
but approach with confidence
to find our home in you
through Jesus Christ, Amen.

Luke 8.41-end
(Mark 5.21-43)
Jairus' daughter/ Woman with the haemorrhage

Pentecost 3

O Christ for whom we search,
our help when help has failed,
give us courage to expose our need
and ask to be made whole;
that, being touched by you,
we may be raised to new life
in the power of your name, Amen.

Pentecost 4

O God, lover of sinners,
you celebrate our return
as a woman rejoices with her friends.
Where we are lost, search us out,
and where we are locked away,
claim us for your own;
that together we may adorn
the beauty of your face,
through Jesus Christ, Amen.

Luke 15.1-10
Parable of the lost coin

Pentecost 5

O God, whom to follow
is to risk our whole lives;
as Ruth and Naomi
loved and held to one another,
abandoning the ways of the past,
so may we also not be divided,
but travel together
into that strange land where you will lead us
through Jesus Christ, Amen.

Ruth 1.8-17

Pentecost 6

God our father,
you disarm our judgement
with your outrageous mercy;
and the punishment we seek
you turn to celebration.
Lift our self-loathing,
and embrace our stubbornness,
that we too may show such fathering
to an embittered world,
through Jesus Christ, Amen.

Luke 15.11-end
The prodigal son

Pentecost 7

God our lover,
in whose arms we are held,
and by whose passion we are known;
require of us also that love
which is filled with longing,
delights in the truth,
and costs not less than everything,
through Jesus Christ, Amen.

Hosea 11.1-9
1 Corinthians 13
Deuteronomy 10.12-11.1
Mark 12.28-34
The great commandment

Luke 6.27-38

Christ our teacher,
you urge us beyond all reason
to love our enemies,
and pray for our oppressors.
May we embrace such folly
not through subservience, but strength;
that unmeasured generosity
may be poured into our lap,
through Jesus Christ, Amen.

Pentecost 8

Ephesians 6.10-20
2 Corinthians 6.3-10

God our security,
who alone can defend us
against the principalities and powers
that rule this present age;
may we trust in no weapons
except the whole armour of faith,
that in dying we may live,
and, having nothing,
we may own the world,
through Jesus Christ, Amen.

Pentecost 9

Luke 7.36-end
Jesus and the woman who loved much
Philippians 2.1-11

Christ Jesus,
whose glory was poured out like perfume,
and who chose for our sake
to take the form of a slave;
may we also pour out our love
with holy extravagance,
that our lives may be fragrant with you,
Amen.

Pentecost 10

2 Corinthians 4.1-10
(2 Timothy 1.7)

O Christ,
to serve whose gospel you have filled us
not with timidity, but power;
help us bear in our body
your wounded humanity;
that we may bodily show forth
your resurrection life,
Amen.

Pentecost 11

Pentecost 12

O God unknown,
in our mother's womb
you formed us for your glory.
Give us a heart to long for you,
grace to discern you,
and courage to proclaim you;
through the one whom you loved
before the foundation of the world,
our saviour Jesus Christ, Amen.

Isaiah 49.1-6
John 17.20-end
Acts 17.22-end
Paul's sermon in Athens
(Jeremiah 1. 4-8)

Pentecost 13

God of truth and terror,
whose word we can with comfort
neither speak nor contain;
give us courage to release the fire
you have shut up in our bones,
and strength in your spirit
to withstand the burning,
through Jesus Christ, Amen.

Jeremiah 20. 7-11
Matthew 10. 16-22

Pentecost 14

God of intimacy,
you surround us with friends and family
to cherish and to challenge.
May we so give and receive caring
in the details of our lives
that we also remain faithful
to your greater demands,
through Jesus Christ, Amen.

Luke 11.1-13
Lord's Prayer/ Friend at midnight

Pentecost 15

Holy God,
by whose authority is judged
all human exercise of power,
give us grace to obey
where we are called to solidarity
and courage to resist
when your justice is at stake,
through Jesus Christ, Amen.

Matthew 14. 1-12
Death of John the Baptist

Leviticus 19.
9-18
Luke 10.25-37
Good Samaritan
1 John 4.15-end
Luke 16.19-end
Rich man and Lazarus

Holy God,
whose name is not honoured
where the needy are not served,
and the powerless are treated with contempt;
may we embrace our neighbour
with the same tenderness
that we ourselves require;
so your justice may be fulfilled in love,
through Jesus Christ, Amen.

Pentecost 16

Jeremiah 32.
6-15
Jeremiah buys the field at Anathoth
Luke 7.1-10
Centurion's servant

God of all trust,
may we who confess your faith
prove it in our lives,
with abundant joy
outrageous hope
and dependence on nothing
but your word alone,
through Jesus Christ, Amen.

Pentecost 17

Ecclesiaticus/
Ben Sirach
38.24-end

God of wholeness,
you have created us bodily,
that our work and faith may be one.
May we offer our worship
from lives of integrity;
and maintain the fabric of this world
with hearts that are set on you,
through Jesus Christ, Amen.

Pentecost 18

Matthew 6.
24-end
Lilies of the field
Romans 5.1-11
Justification by faith

O God, before whose face
we are not made righteous
even by being right;
free us from the need
to justify ourselves
by our own anxious striving,
that we may be abandoned
to faith in you alone,
through Jesus Christ, Amen.

Pentecost 19

Pentecost 20

O God, with whom we wrestle
until the break of day,
make us long to seek your face
beyond the limits of our strength;
that in our wounds we may remember you,
and in your blessing
we may find our selves,
through Jesus Christ, Amen.

Genesis 32. 22-30
Wrestling Jacob

Pentecost 21

Righteous God,
you plead the cause
of the poor and unprotected.
Fill us with holy rage
when justice is delayed,
and give us the persistence
to require those rights that are denied;
for your name's sake, Amen.

Luke 18.1-8
The unjust judge and the persistent widow

Pentecost 22

God of crisis,
you lay before us
either blessing or curse.
In our confusion
give us clarity;
and in our hesitation
the courage to choose boldly
the way that leads to you,
through Jesus Christ, Amen.

Deuteronomy 11.18-28
1 John 2.22-end

Last Sunday in Pentecost

God our desire,
whose coming we look for,
but whose arrival is unexpected;
here in the darkness
make us urgent to greet you,
and open yourself to our longing
that we may be known by you
through Jesus Christ, Amen.

Matthew 25. 1-13
The ten virgins

Some Saints' Days and Festivals

Circumcision of Christ
(January 1)

Luke 2.15-21
(Galatians 3.28)

Christ our brother,
in you there is neither Jew nor Gentile,
neither male nor female;
yet you received the mark of the covenant
and took upon you
the precious burden of the law.
May we so accept in our bodies
our own particular struggle and promise,
that we also may break down barriers
in your name, Amen.

Presentation of Christ
(February 2)

1 Peter 2.1-10
Luke 2.22-35
Jesus is presented in the temple

Christ our cornerstone,
you were recognized at your presentation
as a sign of hope for the world,
but also as a stumbling-block for many;
may we so present our bodies to your service,
that, in sharing your scandal,
we may become a people acceptable to you,
in your name, Amen.

Annunciation
(March 25)
See also Advent 4, p.10

Luke 1.26-38

O God,
you fulfil our desire
beyond what we can bear;
as Mary gave her appalled assent
to your intimate promise,
so may we open ourselves also
to contain your life within us,
through Jesus Christ, Amen.

Julian of Norwich
(May 8)

(Luke 13.34)

Christ our true mother,
you have carried us within you,
laboured with us,
and brought us forth to bliss.
Enclose us in your care,
that in stumbling we may not fall,
nor be overcome by evil,
but know that all shall be well, Amen.

Visitation of Mary to Elizabeth *(May 31)*	**O God our deliverer,** you cast down the mighty, and lift up those of no account; as Elizabeth and Mary embraced with songs of liberation, so may we also be pregnant with your Spirit, and affirm one another in hope for the world, through Jesus Christ, Amen.	Luke 1.39-49
Corpus Christi *(Thursday after Trinity Sunday)*	**O God who took human flesh** that you might be intimate with us; may we so taste and touch you in our bodily life that we may discern and celebrate your body in the world, through Jesus Christ, Amen.	1 Corinthians 11.23-29
Mary Magdalene *(July 22)*	**Christ our healer,** beloved and remembered by women, speak to the grief which makes us forget, and the terror that makes us cling, and give us back our name; that we may greet you clearly, and proclaim your risen life, Amen.	(Luke 8.1-3) *Mary healed by Jesus* John 20.11-18 *Mary at the tomb*
Transfiguration *(August 6)* *Hiroshima Day*	**Christ, our only true light,** before whose bright cloud your friends fell to the ground; we bow before your cross that we may remember in our bodies the dead who fell like shadows; and that we may refuse to be prostrated before the false brightness of any other light, looking to your power alone for hope of resurrection from the dead, Amen.	Luke 9.28-36 (Mark 9.2-13 Matthew 17.1-13) *Transfiguration*

Harvest

Genesis 1.1-3; 24-31
(Genesis 2.4-9
Romans 8. 18-25)

God our creator,
you have made us one with this earth,
to tend it and to bring forth fruit;
may we so respect and cherish
all that has life from you,
that we may share in the labour of all creation
to give birth to your hidden glory,
through Jesus Christ, Amen.

Hilda, Abbess of Whitby
(November 17)

(Jeremiah 1. 4-10)

God our vision,
in our mother's womb
you formed us for your glory.
As your servant Hilda
shone like a jewel in the church
may we now delight to claim her gifts
of judgement and inspiration
reflected in the women of this age,
through Jesus Christ, Amen.

St Andrew
(November 30)

Matthew 4. 12-20
Call of Simon and Andrew
Romans 10. 12-18

Christ, whose insistent call
disturbs our settled lives,
give us discernment to hear your word,
grace to relinquish our tasks,
and courage to follow emptyhanded
wherever you may lead;
that the voice of your gospel
may reach to the ends of the earth,
Amen.

Holy Innocents
(December 28)

Matthew 2. 13-18
Slaughter of the innocents
1 Corinthians 1. 26-29

God of the dispossessed,
defender of the helpless,
you grieve with all the women who weep
because their children are no more;
may we also refuse to be comforted
until the violence of the strong
has been confounded,
and the broken victims have been set free
in the name of Jesus Christ, Amen.

Prayers at times of ending

O God our comfort and challenge,
whose presence is ever reliable
and ever unexpected;
grant us to grieve over what is ending
without falling into despair,
and to enter on our new vocation
without forgetting your voice,
through Jesus Christ, Amen.

Blessing for one laying down office

May the God who rested on the seventh day
to delight in all her creation,
hold you in her arms
as you have held this work,
celebrate with us
the life that takes life from you,
and give you grace to let go
into a new freedom, Amen.

For the dying

O God who brought us to birth,
and in whose arms we die,
we entrust to your embrace
our beloved *sister*.
Give *her* release from *her* pain,
courage to meet the darkness,
and grace to let go into new life,
through Jesus Christ, Amen.

At a funeral

O God who brought us to birth,
and in whose arms we die,
in our grief and shock
contain and comfort us;
embrace us with your love,
give us hope in our confusion,
and grace to let go into new life,
through Jesus Christ, Amen.

Formal
prayers

For the darkness of waiting

For the darkness of waiting
of not knowing what is to come
of staying ready and quiet and attentive,
we praise you O God

**For the darkness and the light
are both alike to you**

For the darkness of staying silent
for the terror of having nothing to say
and for the greater terror
of needing to say nothing,
we praise you O God

**For the darkness and the light
are both alike to you**

For the darkness of loving
in which it is safe to surrender
to let go of our self-protection
and to stop holding back our desire,
we praise you O God

**For the darkness and the light
are both alike to you**

For the darkness of choosing
when you give us the moment
to speak, and act, and change,
and we cannot know what we have set in motion,
but we still have to take the risk,
we praise you O God

**For the darkness and the light
are both alike to you**

For the darkness of hoping
in a world which longs for you,
for the wrestling and the labouring of all creation
for wholeness and justice and freedom,
we praise you O God

**For the darkness and the light
are both alike to you.**

First written for the *Women in Theology* liturgy group, Advent Sunday, 1985, this litany was also used in the *Liturgy of Hope*, Canterbury Cathedral, 18 April 1986.

Hymn to Wisdom

This hymn was written as a reflection upon a meeting of the *Peace Preaching Course*, on the theme *'And the Word was made flesh'*, held in Oxford, July 1987.

It may be read antiphonally, each voice taking two lines alternately.

My soul yearns for wisdom,
and beyond all else my heart longs for her.
She has walked through the depths of the abyss,
she has measured its boundaries;
for she was there from the beginning,
and apart from her, not one thing came to be.
She played before creation, when the world was made,
and in her hands are all things held together;
she has danced upon the face of the deep,
and all that has breath is instinct with her life.
The mystery of creation is in her grasp,
yet she delights to expound her ways.

In the streets of the city, wisdom is calling,
and on the access roads she encounters those who pass;
at the gates of the camp she sings in triumph,
and in the law courts she lifts up her voice.
With the timid and fearful she takes her stand,
and in the mouths of children she is heard to speak.
She cries out to the foolish to listen,
and the wise take heed to her words.
But among her own, she is not recognized,
and those who need her have thrust her out;
she has been pushed aside like the poor,
and broken like those of no account.

So she abandons those who are wise in their own sight,
but with all who are ready to receive her,
she makes her home.
For her delight is in the truth,
and she takes no pleasure in deceitful ways;
her integrity is more to be desired than comfort,
and her discernment is more precious than security.
In her alone is the life of humanity,
therefore while I live I will search her out;
for whoever is fed by wisdom will never hunger,
and all who drink from her will never thirst again.

Statement of faith

O God, the source of our being
and the goal of all our longing,
we believe and trust in you.
The whole earth is alive with your glory,
and all that has life is sustained by you.
We commit ourselves to cherish your world,
and to seek your face.

O God, embodied in a human life,
we believe and trust in you.
Jesus our brother, born of the woman Mary,
you confronted the proud and the powerful,
and welcomed as your friends
those of no account.
Holy Wisdom of God, firstborn of creation,
you emptied yourself of power,
and became foolishness for our sake.
You laboured with us upon the cross,
and have brought us forth
to the hope of resurrection.
We commit ourselves to struggle against evil
and to choose life.

O God, life-giving Spirit,
Spirit of healing and comfort,
of integrity and truth,
we believe and trust in you.
Warm-winged Spirit, brooding over creation,
rushing wind and Pentecostal fire,
we commit ourselves to work with you
and renew our world.

This statement of faith, and the confession that follows, were written and revised for regular use in the *Women in Theology* liturgy group.

Confession and mutual absolution

O God, you have searched us out and known us,
and all that we are is open to you.
We confess that we have sinned:
we have used our power to dominate
and our weakness to manipulate;
we have evaded responsibility
and failed to confront evil;
we have denied dignity
to ourselves and to our sisters *(each other),*
and fallen into despair.

We turn to you, O God;
we renounce evil;
we claim your love;
we choose to be made whole.

(In turn, around the circle, we say for each other: 'Woman/man, your sins are forgiven; be at peace.'
This can be accompanied by a gesture such as taking hands, or making the sign of the cross on the forehead.)

Litany of penitence for the denial of women's authority

This litany and the one that follows were written for a festival service to mark the opening of holy orders to women in the Diocese of London, on 31 March 1987, at the church of St Mary-le-Bow. During the confession, spoken by the congregation, the new women deacons were enclosed in a side-chapel, and processed out to receive the blessing.

Man: Let us confess our sins:
We have denied the authority of women
and limited their gifts;
we have locked away women's power,
and chosen to hide their pain.
But nothing is veiled that will not be revealed;

Men: And nothing is hidden
that will not be made known.

Woman: We have undermined the authority of women
and limited our gifts;
we have locked away women's power,
and chosen to hide our pain.
But nothing is veiled that will not be revealed;

Women: And nothing is hidden
that will not be made known.

Man: We have feared those who are not like us;
we have refused to know our weakness.
We have locked away part of ourselves.
But nothing is veiled that will not be revealed;

Men: And nothing is hidden
that will not be made known.

Woman: We have feared those who are like us;
we have refused to know our strength.
We have locked away part of ourselves.
But nothing is veiled that will not be revealed;

Women: And nothing is hidden
that will not be made known.

Man: We have resisted the Wisdom of God
and refused to seek her face.

Woman: We have turned aside from her image
and hidden our knowledge of her.
But have no fear:
for nothing is veiled that will not be revealed;

All: And nothing is hidden
that will not be made known.

Litany of blessing for women taking authority

Woman: Blessed is she who believed there would be a fulfilment of what was spoken to her by the Lord.

Women: Blessed are you among women.

Man: May you speak with the voice of the voiceless, and give courage to those in despair.

Men: Blessed are you among women.

Woman: May you feed the hungry of mind and heart, and send away satisfied those who are empty.

Women: Blessed are you among women.

Man: May you be strong to confront injustice, and powerful to rebuke the arrogant.

Men: Blessed are you among women.

Woman: May you not be alone, but find support in your struggle, and sisters to rejoice with you.

Women: Blessed are you among women.

Man: May your vision be fulfilled, in company with us; may you have brothers on your journey.

Men: Blessed are you among women.

Woman: Blessed is she who believed there would be a fulfilment of what was spoken to her by the Lord.

All: Blessed are you among women.

Eucharistic prayer for ordinary use

Eternal Wisdom, source of our being,
and goal of all our longing,
we praise you and give you thanks
because you have created us, women and men,
together in your image
to cherish your world and seek your face.
Divided and disfigured by sin,
while we were yet helpless,
you emptied yourself of power,
and took upon you our unprotected flesh.
You laboured with us upon the cross,
and have brought us forth
to the hope of resurrection.

Therefore, with the woman who gave you birth,
the women who befriended you and fed you,
who argued with you and touched you,
the woman who anointed you for death,
the women who met you, risen from the dead,
and with all your lovers throughout the ages,
we praise you saying:

Holy, holy, holy,
vulnerable God,
heaven and earth are full of your glory;
hosanna in the highest.
Blessed is the one
who comes in the name of God;
hosanna in the highest.

Blessed is our brother Jesus,
who, before his suffering, earnestly desired
to eat with his companions
the passover of liberation;
who, on the night that he was betrayed,
took bread, gave thanks, broke it, and said:
'This is my body, which is for you.
Do this to remember me.'

In the same way also the cup, after supper,
saying:
'This cup is the new covenant in my blood.
Do this, whenever you drink it,
to remember me.'

Christ has died.
Christ is risen.
Christ will come again.

Therefore, as we eat this bread and drink this cup,
we are proclaiming Christ's death until he comes.
In the body broken and the blood poured out,
we restore to memory and hope
the broken and unremembered victims
of tyranny and sin;
and we long for the bread of tomorrow
and the wine of the age to come.
Come then, life-giving spirit of our God,
brood over these bodily things,
and make us one body with Christ;
that we may labour with creation
to be delivered from its bondage to decay
into the glorious liberty
of all the children of God.

Eucharistic prayer for Chistmas Eve

This prayer was written for a eucharistic celebration on Christmas Eve 1986, at Holy Trinity House, Paddington, attended only by women. A woman priest presided. The poem at the end of the collection, *That night, we gathered for the birth,* was written after this occasion.

O Eternal Wisdom,
we praise you and give you thanks,
because you emptied yourself of power
and became foolishness for our sake;
for on this night you were delivered as one of us,
a baby needy and naked,
wrapped in a woman's blood;
born into poverty and exile,
to proclaim the good news to the poor,
and to let the broken victims go free.

Therefore, with the woman who gave you birth,
the women who befriended you and fed you,
who argued with you and touched you,
the woman who anointed you for death,
the women who met you, risen from the dead,
and with all your lovers throughout the ages,
we praise you, saying:

Holy, holy, holy,
vulnerable God,
heaven and earth are full of your glory;
hosanna in the highest.
Blessed is the one
who comes in the name of God;
hosanna in the highest.

Blessed is our brother Jesus,
bone of our bone and flesh of our flesh;
who, on the night when he was delivered over to death,
took bread, gave thanks, broke it, and said:
'This is my body, which is for you.
Do this to remember me.'
In the same way also the cup, after supper, saying:
'This cup is the new covenant in my blood.
Do this, whenever you drink it,

to remember me.'
For, as we eat this bread and drink this cup,
we are proclaiming the Lord's death until he
comes.

Christ has died.
Christ is risen.
Christ will come again.

Come now, dearest Spirit of God,
embrace us with your comfortable power.
Brood over these bodily things,
and make us one body in Christ.
As Mary's body was broken for him,
and her blood shed,
so may we show forth his brokenness
for the life of the world,
and may creation be made whole
through the new birth in his blood.

Footwashing liturgy for Maundy Thursday

O Eternal Wisdom,
we praise you and give you thanks,
because you laid aside your power as a garment,
and took upon you the form of a slave.
You became obedient unto death,
even death on a cross,
receiving authority and comfort
from the hands of a woman;
for God chose what is weak in the world
to shame the strong,
and God chose what is low and despised in the world,
even things that are not,
to bring to nothing things that are.

Therefore, with the woman who gave you birth,
the women who befriended you and fed you,
who argued with you and touched you,
the woman who anointed you for death,
the women who met you, risen from the dead,
and with all your lovers throughout the ages,
we praise you saying:

Holy, holy, holy,
vulnerable God,
heaven and earth are full of your glory;
hosanna in the highest.
Blessed is the one
who comes in the name of God;
hosanna in the highest.

Blessed is our brother Jesus,
who on this night, before Passover,
rose from supper, laid aside his garments,
took a towel and poured water,
and washed his disciples' feet, saying to them:
'If I, your Lord and Teacher,
have washed your feet,

This liturgy was first used at the Greenham vigil, on Maundy Thursday 1987, by a group of Christian women at Blue Gate, Greenham Common. It was followed by a Passover meal.

you also ought to wash one another's feet.
If you know these things,
blessed are you if you do them.
If I do not wash you,
you have no part in me.'

Lord, not my feet only
but also my hands and my head.

Come now, tender spirit of our God,
wash us and make us one body in Christ;
that, as we are bound together
in this gesture of love,
we may no longer be in bondage
to the principalities and powers
that enslave creation,
but may know your liberating peace
such as the world cannot give.

(This prayer is followed by the
mutual washing of feet)

Eucharistic prayer for Easter

O Eternal Wisdom,
we praise you and give you thanks,
because the beauty of death
could not contain you.
You broke forth from the comfort of the grave;
before you the stone was moved,
and the tomb of our world was opened wide.
For on this day you were raised in power
and revealed yourself to women
as a beloved stranger,
offering for the rituals of the dead
the terror of new life
and of desire fulfilled.

Therefore, with the woman who gave you birth,
the women who befriended you and fed you,
who argued with you and touched you,
the woman who anointed you for death,
the women who met you, risen from the dead,
and with all your lovers throughout the ages,
we praise you, saying:

Holy, holy, holy,
resurrection God,
heaven and earth are full of your glory;
hosanna in the highest.
Blessed is the one
who comes in the name of God;
hosanna in the highest.

Blessed is our brother Jesus,
who walks with us the road of our grief,
and is known again in the breaking of bread;
who, on the night he was handed over,
took bread, gave thanks, broke it, and said:
'This is my body, which is for you.
Do this to remember me.'
In the same way also the cup, after supper,

This prayer was written for the St Hilda Community in East London, a mixed group of women and men who worship regularly together, and whose particular concern is to affirm and celebrate the ministry of women. It was first used on Easter Day, 1987.

saying:
'This cup is the new covenant in my blood.
Do this whenever you drink it,
to remember me.'

Christ has died.
Christ is risen.
Christ will come again.

Come now, disturbing spirit of our God,
breathe on these bodily things
and make us one body in Christ.
Open our graves, unbind our eyes,
and name us here;
touch and heal all that has been buried in us,
that we need not cling to our pain,
but may go forth with power
to release resurrection in the world.

Eucharistic prayer for Pentecost

O Eternal Wisdom,
we praise you and give you thanks,
for, as you revealed yourself of old
in fire and storm and precious law,
so you did not leave your followers comfortless,
but came upon them on this day
in thunder, wind and flame,
filling them with clarity and power,
and making them drunk with longing
to utter your uncontainable word.
And now, you have poured out your spirit
upon all flesh,
that your sons and daughters may prophesy,
that old and young may share a vision,
and even the slaves find a voice.

Therefore,
with Elizabeth who prophesied your birth,
Mary who sang for the poor,
Martha who confessed you as the Christ,
the women who announced you
risen from the dead,
and with every nameless and unremembered
prophet
who heard your call and inspired her people,
we praise you, saying:

Holy, holy, holy,
God of power and might,
heaven and earth are full of your glory;
hosanna in the highest.
Blessed is the one
who comes in the name of God;
hosanna in the highest.

Blessed is our brother Jesus,
who comes behind the doors we have closed,

This prayer was written for the St Hilda Community. It was first used at Pentecost, 1987.

and breathes on our fear his fearful peace;
who, on the night that he was betrayed,
took bread, gave thanks, broke it, and said:
'This is my body, which is for you.
Do this to remember me.'
In the same way the cup, after supper, saying:
'This cup is the new covenant in my blood.
Do this whenever you drink it,
to remember me.'

We remember Christ's death;
we proclaim Christ's resurrection;
we await Christ's coming in glory.

Come now, spirit of integrity,
of tenderness, judgement, and dance;
touch our speechlessness,
kindle our longing,
reach into our silence,
and fire our words with your truth;
that each may hear in her own language
the mighty works of God.

Benedicite omnia opera

All you works of God, bless your creator;
praise her and glorify her for ever.

Let the wide earth bless the creator;
let the arching heavens bless the creator;
let the whole body of God bless the creator;
praise her and glorify her for ever.

You returning daylight, bless your creator;
twilight and shadows, bless your creator;
embracing darkness, bless your creator;
praise her and glorify her for ever.

Mountains of God, massive and ancient rocks,
bless your creator;
valleys and pastures, moorland and rivers,
bless your creator;
ocean depths and lonely abyss,
bless your creator;
praise her and glorify her for ever.

Storm and mighty wind, bless your creator;
bitter cold and scorching sun, bless your creator;
mist and cloud and tender rain,
bless your creator;
praise her and glorify her for ever.

Seed and sapling, tree and vivid flower,
bless your creator;
greenness and flourishing,
withering and bareness, bless your creator;
harvest and springtime and deadness of the year,
bless your creator;
praise her and glorify her for ever.

You creatures of God, bless your creator;
swift and cunning, violent and graceful,
bless your creator;

This canticle was first used at the Greenham vigil, August 1987.

all who creep and soar and dance across the earth,
bless your creator;
praise her and glorify her for ever.

You newborn babies, bless your creator;
young and old, mature and aging,
bless your creator;
all you dying, bless your creator;
praise her and glorify her for ever.

In pain and desolation, let us bless our creator;
in the place of delight, let us bless our creator;
in time of waiting, let us bless our creator;
praise her and glorify her for ever.

Let all who live and grow and breathe
bless our creator,
praise her and glorify her for ever.

Blessings

O God our dance,
in whom we live and move and have our being;
so direct our strength
and inspire our weakness
that we may enter with power
into the movement of your whole creation,
through our partner Jesus Christ, Amen.

May holy Wisdom,
kind to humanity,
steadfast, sure and free,
the breath of the power of God;
may she who makes all things new, in every age,
enter our souls,
and make us friends of God,
through Jesus Christ, Amen.

Easter

May the God who shakes heaven and earth,
whom death could not contain,
who lives to disturb and heal us,
bless you with power to go forth
and proclaim the gospel,
Amen.

Pentecost

May the God who dances in creation,
who embraces us with human love,
who shakes our lives like thunder,
bless us and drive us out with power
to fill the world with her justice,
Amen.

Psalms and Poems

I will praise God, my Beloved

I will praise God, my Beloved,
for she is altogether lovely.

Her presence satisfies my soul;
she fills my senses to overflowing
so that I cannot speak.

Her touch brings me to life;
the warmth of her hands makes me wholly alive.

Her embrace nourishes me, body and spirit;
every part of my being responds to her touch.

The beauty of her face is more than I can bear;
in her gaze I drown.

When she looks upon me
I can withold nothing;

when she asks for my love
all my defences crumble;
my pride and my control are utterly dissolved.

O God I fear your terrible mercy;
I am afraid to surrender my self.

If I let go into the whirlpool of your love,
shall I survive the embrace?

If I fall into the strong currents of your desire,
shall I escape drowning?

But how shall I refuse my Beloved,
and how can I withdraw from the one my heart yearns for?

On the edge of your abyss I look down and I tremble;
but I will not stand gazing for ever.

Even in chaos you will bear me up;
if the waters go over my head,
you will still be holding me.

For the chaos is yours also,
and in the swirling of mighty waters
is your presence known.

If I trust her, surely her power will not fail me;
nor will she let me be utterly destroyed.

Though I lose all knowledge and all security,
yet will my God never forsake me;

but she will recreate me, in her steadfast love,
so that I need not be afraid.

Then will I praise my Beloved among the people,
among those who seek to know God.

God my God, why have you deserted me?

God my God, why have you deserted me?
Why do I lie awake pleading,
when there is no-one to hear me?

For my longing is more than I can bear,
my loneliness is like a yawning pit,
and my hunger is not filled.

For I said, I will seek my God and know her,
and she will answer me, and I shall be satisfied.

Behold, your word was before me and I sought you,
you opened my heart, so that I could not refuse your touch.
You reached your hand into the depths and drew me;
and my body flowed out with love.
I was given to you, body and soul;
I tendered my spirit and I held nothing back.

But you have seduced me O God, and I was seduced.
When I reached out to touch you,
my hands grasped emptiness;
I stretched out my arms and my heart,
and there was nothing to hold.

Why have I trusted in your word, O God?
Your word has become an agony to me,
and I cannot put it aside;
my mind searches it continually, but I find no rest.

But how can I say, I will forget her compassion;
and how can I return to my self,
as if her love had never been?
For the floods have passed through me,
and I have been changed;
the channels and gulleys remember the waters,
and they mourn;
the narrow places of my soul do not cease to hope for rain.

So I will remember my God, though she is far from me;
and though there is no-one to hold me,
yet will I hold my heart open.

God is my strong rock in whom I trust

God is my strong rock in whom I trust,
and all my confidence I rest in her.

Deep in my mother's womb, she knew me;
before my limbs were formed, she yearned for me.
Each of my movements she remembers with compassion,
and when I wás still unseen, she did imagine me.

Her strength brought me forth into the light;
it was she who delivered me.
Hers were the hands that held me safe;
she cherished me upon my mother's breast.

When I stammer, she forms the words in my mouth,
and when I am silent, she has understood my thoughts.
If I shout and rage, she hears my plea and my uncertainty.

When I am afraid, she stays close to me,
and when I am full of terror, she does not hide her face.
If I struggle against her, she will contain me,
and when I resist her, she will match my strength.

But if I am complacent, she confronts me;
when I cling to falsehood, she undermines my pride;
for she is jealous for my integrity,
and her longing is for nothing less than truth.

To all who are weak she shows compassion,
and those who are downtrodden she causes to rise.
But she will confound the arrogant
at the height of their power,
and the oppressor she will throw to the ground;
the strategies of the hard-hearted she will utterly confute.

God pities the fallen, and I will love her;
she challenges the mighty,
and I desire her with my whole heart.
God is the rock in whom I put my trust,
and all my meaning is contained in her;
for without God there is no security,
and apart from her there is no place of safety.

As a woman in labour who longs for the birth

As a woman in labour who longs for the birth,
I long for you, O God;
and as she is weary to see the face of her child,
so do I seek your deliverance.
She cries out, she pants, because her pain is great,
and her longing is beyond measure;
her whole body is groaning in travail
until she shall be delivered.

My soul hungers for you
as the child for her mother's breast;
like the infant who cries out in the night,
who waits in the dark to be comforted.
At night I will cry for your justice,
and in the morning I will seek you early;
for you O God are the source of my salvation,
and all my nourishment is found in you.

As a woman looks to her friend,
that she may open her heart and be free,
that her words may find understanding,
and her fears may be contained;
so do I look to you O God,
that you may search me and know my ways,
bringing me judgement and tenderness,
and sending me home released.

As the body of the lover yearns for her beloved,
so is my desire for your touch.
She cries out from her depths, she weeps,
and cannot speak
because of the beauty of her beloved.
You also have laid your hand upon me,
and I cannot forget your ways.

So I will cry for my Beloved, and I will not rest,
until I dwell in the darkness of her embrace,
and all my silence is enclosed in her.

They have taken away my Lord

John 20.1-18
Mary Magdalene at the tomb

It was unfinished.
We stayed there, fixed, until the end,
women waiting for the body that we loved;
and then it was unfinished.
There was no time to cherish, cleanse, anoint;
no time to handle him with love,
no farewell.

Since then, my hands have waited,
aching to touch even his deadness,
smoothe oil into bruises that no longer hurt,
offer his silent flesh my finished act of love.

I came early, as the darkness lifted,
to find the grave ripped open and his body gone;
container of my grief smashed, looted,
leaving my hands still empty.
I turned on the man who came:
'They have taken away my Lord—where is his corpse?
Where is the body that is mine to greet?
He is not gone
I am not ready yet, I am not finished—
I cannot let him go
I am not whole.'

And then he spoke, no corpse,
and breathed,
and offered me my name.
My hands rushed to grasp him;
to hold and hug and grip his body close;
to give myself again, to cling to him,
and lose my self in love.
'Don't touch me now.'

I stopped, and waited, my rejected passion
hovering between us like some dying thing.
I, Mary, stood and grieved, and then departed.

I have a gospel to proclaim.

In darkness and anxiety
I searched for her continually,
treading again the paths of my confusion,
knowing I know nothing.

In darkness and aridity
I longed for her variety,
absorbed and aching with my neediness,
feeling I know nothing.

In darkness and in emptiness
I pleaded for her tenderness,
fingering the pain of my familiar loss,
fearing to know nothing.

In darkness and in urgency
I courted her insistently,
leaning towards the kisses of her mouth,
yearning to know nothing.

In darkness and obscurity
I waited for her secretly,
learning to hide the face of my desire,
choosing to know nothing.

In darkness and security
she came to me abundantly,
touching the speechless and reluctant part of me
needing to know nothing.

and you held me

and you held me and there were no words
and there was no time and you held me
and there was only wanting and
being held and being filled with wanting
and I was nothing but letting go
and being held
and there were no words and there
needed to be no words
and there was no terror   only stillness
and I was wanting nothing and
it was fullness and it was like aching for God
and it was touch and warmth and
darkness and no time and no words and we flowed
and I flowed and I was not empty
and I was given up to the dark and
in the darkness   I was not lost
and the wanting was like fullness and I could
hardly hold it and I was held and
you were dark and warm and without time and
without words and you held me

That night we gathered for the birth, as women
have always done—as women
have never done till now;
and in an ordinary room,
warm, exposed, and intimate as childbed,
we spoke about our bodies and our blood,
waiting for God's delivery:
silence, gesture, and speech
announcing, with a strange appropriate blend
of mystery and bluntness,
the celebration of the word made flesh
midwived wholly by women.

The following items first appeared in Janet Morley and Hannah Ward (eds), **Celebrating Women** (Morehouse-Barlow, 1988):

'For the darkness of waiting'
Collects:
8 before Easter
Lent 4
Easter Day 'O God, the power of the powerless'
Pentecost 5
Visitation
Harvest

The psalm 'God is my strong rock in whom I trust' first appeared in **The Month,** February 1988.

The aim of the
Movement for the Ordination of Women (MOW)
is to promote the ordination of women in the Anglican churches of the British Isles, as a fundamental part of the ministry of women and men in the church.

Women in Theology (WIT)
is a national network concerned to build women-centered community through a range of educational and liturgical activities for those wanting to do theology from a feminist perspective.

73184